Daily Listening:
A Summer of Reflection

A Collection of Meditations for Your Spirit

A Publication of Well for the Journey, Inc.

VISION

Gathering...
  Seeking the Source of Wholeness and Life
    Longing to Quench a Common Thirst
      Nurturing One Another.
In Community...
  Being Filled and Renewed
    Becoming Living Water
      For Others in the World.

MISSION

In response to God's grace and spirit, The Well offers spiritual nourishment for daily living. Though grounded in Christianity, the center reaches beyond denominations and traditions to provide opportunities for spiritual growth and formation, equipping individuals to serve God and others.

Daily Listening: *A Summer of Reflection*
ISBN: 978-0-9829126-1-4
Copyright© 2011
Well for the Journey Publishing
2nd Edition

Well for the Journey Publishing
a division of Well for the Journey, Inc.
7600 York Road
Towson, MD 21204
410-296-9355
www.wellforjourney.org
Email: info@wellforjourney.org

Various translations of the Holy Bible are used throughout the text. For details on the translation, please refer to the citations, found on pages 86 through 90.

Introduction

Summer is often a Sabbath time—a time to slow down, retreat from the busyness of life (if only for a short while!), and spend some time in quiet reflection. Well for the Journey, Inc. (The Well) is delighted to offer *Daily Listening: A Summer of Reflection* as a resource for spiritual nourishment and reflection during the summer months.

Listening is the most human of activities. The leisure days of summer offer us ample opportunity to listen and to celebrate life as a divine gift. As you move through the pages of *Daily Listening,* we invite you to begin each week with a brief guided reflection...to ponder the quotes and reflections...to journal your thoughts and feelings...and to revisit the guided reflection at week's end to see and celebrate how God is at work in you.

This book is a compilation of real-life meditations written by friends of The Well. The writers and editors took great care to offer reflections that speak broadly about our encounters with God and the spiritual life. In order to address the wide diversity of approaches to the divine presence, it seems important to offer a few comments about the names we use to refer to "God." Each one of us has an individual, unique relationship with God, and many of us have our preferred name for our God. God may be "Father," "Mother," "Holy One," "Divine Power;" or simply unnamed. In order to offer a unifying tone to this book, as well as to recognize that our names for God are uniquely our own preference, we have decided, whenever possible, to use the recognized gender-neutral name "God." We hope that when you read the word "God," you will substitute the name that best suits your relationship with God.

My prayer is that *Daily Listening: A Summer of Reflection* will speak to you in a deep and meaningful way.

Wishing you summer Sabbath blessings,
Kathy Baker
Project Director
Daily Listening: A Summer of Reflection

Using this Book

Daily Listening: A Summer of Reflection is designed to be a daily resource for spiritual nourishment. The book is organized in seven-day cycles centered on a specific theme related to the spiritual life. On the first day, you are gently introduced to the week's theme by the word "Pondering..." followed by questions which invite you to ponder the theme and consider how it relates to your life. For the next five days, you are offered quotes and reflections that resonate with the theme. The final day of the week begins with the words "Echoes of..." This is a day to listen for the echoes of what you have experienced during the previous six days, and to discover and celebrate how God is at work in you. There is space on each page to write down your thoughts if you so desire.

Pondering . . . A Listening Heart

Where your treasure is, there your heart will be also.
(Matthew 6:21, NRSV)

The heart is the true listener within us.
What does it mean for you to listen with your heart?
What hopes are contained in your heart?

This week, listen to your heart and let it lead you!

God speaks to us every day only
we don't know how to listen.

— Mahatma Gandhi

Our modern and multitasked world conspires to keep us from listening—to God or to others. Also, when we are preoccupied with ourselves, we are often better at "broadcasting" our point of view than "receiving" from others. Some of our best listening takes place as a part of a dialogue. True dialogue occurs when we move beyond ourselves to an authentic relationship with God or another person.

Hearing God's voice, and discerning God's will, comes to us in many forms and through many of our senses. We can stop and heighten our sensitivities and abilities to hear and "receive" by giving God and others the precious gift of our very real and undivided attention. In this sense, active listening is inextricably linked to active loving. When we reach out to God and to others in love, we can hear God speak to us. I often pray simply for the ability to bring God to, and to find God in, relationships with others, and the beauty of the natural world around me.

Be still, and know that I am God.

— Psalm 46:10 (NIV)

Years ago, I learned to pray this psalm verse slowly, hoping it would move me deep into the center of my being. Slowly I would pray:
    Be still and know that I am God......then,
        after several minutes, I would pray:
    Be still and know that I am...........then:
    Be still and know.....................then:
    Be still...................................and finally
    Be....
    This is where I would lose it!
    It is so hard to just BE before the God who loves us.
    Minds race, and there is so much for us to DO.

I wonder, if I listen again and again and more deeply, might I hear these same words in the way that a mother speaks to her restless child held in her arms..."just be still...just be still...be still....be..."?

Loving God, still my being!

*. . . allow yourself to be present, without imposing or
demanding, to hold a space where something can be told,
where a meeting can unfold, where openness is answered.*

— Llewellyn Vaughan-Lee

Sitting by a bedside is so often like that—just being present—or at
least it ought to be. I am not "I" so much as I am an undemanding but
alert and active presence. I am in expectation, but I need not make
anything happen. I am in expectation, but I have no expectations. I
wait. If the patient is asleep, I may pray, or read the psalms, or sing
softly. If the patient is awake, we may talk—or not; I may sing—or not.
But always, I think, I am praying.

Something will unfold, something will flower, something will breathe
through the attentiveness. I need not strive; I need only be alert. I
need only be ready for the moment when God's breath mingles with
our breaths, and truth happens.

June 4

Bring me to the silence within myself,
and give me comfort there. Show me the fierce
and quiet center of Your love, which is within me.

— Marianne Williamson

Listen with the ear of your heart.

— St. Benedict

As I approached the door of my son's home where I was to meet his bride's transgender sister, I thought about the time I had spent in reflective prayer, preparing for this meeting. Conflicting values waged war within me. I finally concluded that it was not my place to judge. If I truly wanted to imitate Jesus, then I must show it in my actions. I was determined to treat her with kindness and respect. A small part of me was worried. Would I feel repelled, confused, or uncomfortable? If so, would the look on my face betray me? Instead, the power of grace touched my heart.

When our eyes met, I felt a flood of compassion rise from deep within my heart. I could see the hesitation in her eyes as she searched mine to see my reaction. To think of the injustices she had suffered at the words, hands, and actions of others made me feel ashamed. We are all one body in Christ. When one member hurts, we all hurt. Yet, when one member loves another, we are all touched by grace. If we truly desire to love our neighbor as ourselves, God will transform our hearts so our actions reflect God's love to others. Blessed be the Lord.

June 6

Echoes of . . . A Listening Heart

Where your treasure is, there your heart will be also.
(Matthew 6:21, NRSV)

Thinking back on this week,
    What did it mean for you to listen with your heart?
    When did your heart lead you? Where did it lead you?
    What treasures did you discover?

June 7

Pondering . . . Nature

God speaks through all of nature.

How do you experience God while you are amidst nature?
Which aspects of nature most connect you with the Sacred?
What does nature teach you about your relationship with God?
    About all of life?

Each day this week, spend time in nature. Listen...what do you hear?

There are times when we stop. We sit still...
We listen and breezes from a whole other
world begin to whisper.

— James Carroll

It's hard to remember exactly when I began sitting in my car waiting for my daughter during her piano lesson, but it's probably been about four years. I put the seat back, kick off my shoes, gaze at the sky, and daydream. I sit still and listen. It must be an odd sight to see a middle-aged woman sitting in a parked car, in a city neighborhood, where the trees form a beautiful canopy.

Only once did someone stop to ask, "What are you doing here?" It was a white-haired woman, whose tone was hostile and who didn't care for my response about the piano teacher and lessons. She became agitated that I wasn't wearing shoes, and I later learned that she had Alzheimer's disease. But, she is the one who stopped and allowed me a glimpse into her world.

It is difficult to step into another's world, especially an unfamiliar or painful one, such as this woman's world seemed to be. Her mind caused her to stop and notice something that was out of place—me.

What does it take to stop, sit still, and listen, and to reach out of our own world into another's with a helpful hand or a kind word?

There are occasions when you can hear the mysterious language of the Earth, in water...coming through the trees... through the undercurrents of the soil; but you have to be willing to wait and receive.

— John Hay

There is a place
at the center of everything

Where heart meets heart
and love lives

Where knowledge means nothing
and understanding is all

Let us meet there
from time to time

Perhaps when a tree's majesty
reminds us of our smallness

Or when the trill of a bird
delights our ear

All creation teaches us some way of prayer.

—Thomas Merton

Creation is vast, the world and everything in it. Each annunciation in this great exterior summons the interior. God gestures, invites us to notice, and desires our response. The moment when external and internal intermingle in pure and shared presence, the womb of prayer is fashioned. From this divine encounter, we are with prayer, as mother is with child. At times, we undermine this summoning. We abort our innate response to nurture this sacred call. We are not available to creation, to our true self, nor to our God.

Through grace and reconciliation, our awareness returns. God loves us into fullness through every experience. Our each and every interior impression is content for our blessed exchange. Tension dissolves between our doing and being, light and dark, dependence and independence. We become heavy with prayer as our reliance on our Creator meets our unequivocal uniqueness in truth. Pregnant with mutual adoration, the interior and exterior co-create. From the womb of prayer, through holy co-laboring, creation bursts forth.

Magnificently, from conception to birth, freedom realized, love delivered with faith and hope blossoming boundlessly, now gift for others.

> *I don't know exactly what a prayer is. I do know how to pay*
> *attention, how to fall down into the grass, how to kneel*
> *down in the grass, how to be idle and blessed . . .*
>
> — Mary Oliver

Walking in the woods. The practice began as an escape—from the noise in my head, the stress of my work, and an ache in my heart—justified as necessary physical exercise, exactly the kind of "doing" I was good at. Over the weeks and months, however, my pace slowed. My gaze was drawn upward to track the course of a pileated woodpecker nearing its nesting tree. My ears were trained to the chatter of titmice gathered in the underbrush seeking protection from the winter winds. I followed the circuitous path of fox tracks in new-fallen snow. I learned just when in April to see the coiling of the mating carp. I knew the green-gold hue of the woods in early spring and the heavy humus-scented moisture of July after a thunderstorm. The woods taught me how to pay attention and how to be idle, precisely the lessons I needed to enter into the prayer of being that I now know is spoken continuously. Thank You, thank You, thank You.

For God alone my soul waits in silence.

— Psalm 62:5 (NRSV)

Waiting is such a human activity, and for us in our fast-paced living, often a very frustrating one! We wait in check-out lines, at traffic lights, "on hold" on the phone, for the economy to shift. We wait for medical test results, for suffering to pass. We wait for babies to be born, and for loved ones to die, only to be reborn to a new life.

The hardest times of waiting for me are those times when it is only for God that I can wait. All my human efforts, resources, and ways have been tried to no avail. Now the situation is in God's hands and I can only wait...alone and in silence. It is the words of T.S. Eliot that help my waiting: "I said to my soul, be still, and wait without hope, for hope would be hope for the wrong thing; wait without love, for love would be love of the wrong thing; there is yet faith, but the faith and the love and the hope are all in the waiting....So the darkness shall be light, and the stillness the dancing."

June 13

Echoes of . . . Nature

God speaks through all of nature.

Thinking back on this week,
>   How did you experience God in nature this past week?
>   Which aspects of nature most connected you with
>   the Sacred?
>   What did nature teach you about your relationship with God?
>   About all of life?

June 14

Pondering . . . Possibility

Dwell in possibility.

What helps you to become more open to possibility?
What possibilities are calling to you?
What might it be like for you to listen and live wide open?

As you listen this week, be more attuned to what is possible, rather
than to what is certain or wrong.

> *Everything has its wonders, even darkness and silence,*
> *and I learn, whatever state I may be in, therein*
> *to be content.*
>
> — Helen Keller

Compared to Helen Keller's life—my life, alive with sight and sound, has been easy. Nevertheless, I too have known the "darkness and silence" of hard times. In the spring of 2003, life as I'd known it was falling apart. My marriage of 32 years hung by a thread that would soon break in two. A change of career was necessary and stirred feelings of inadequacy and angst. And Baxter, my Labrador retriever, was dying.

I look back wondering how I kept my balance at all...how I resisted curling up in a permanent fetal position. Surely, it was only by the grace of God, grace presented and experienced daily in uncountable small wonders. My part was to be present, listening with all my being—ears, eyes, nose, touch—and my heart. It became a spiritual discipline and a lifeline to God. Each day brought reminders that God was in the thick of it with me—the sound of hummingbird wings, the cat cuddling close, the smell of spaghetti sauce simmering, an early morning sky replete with fading moon and rising sun. Through wonders such as these, I encountered contentment, and it has reshaped my life.

June 16

What I tell you in the dark, speak in daylight; what is whispered in your ear, proclaim from the roofs.

— Matthew 10:27 (NIV)

Flashlight in Hand

At dusk and at dawn I think God is a small child
Sprawled on the grass with a flashlight in hand
Illuminating the yard, with a tilted elbow, and a sparkling smile

In the morning, as I rub my eyes and venture out
God whispers "Look at that!"
The golden trees, the perfect spider webs
The dew on grass, the purple mountains
And finally that silhouette of a horizon

God is showing me direction, saying, "Go forward"
God is showing me my dreams, divine hope
My possibilities

When wearily I return at dusk
God's flashlight is more a reminder
No matter what has occurred
No matter what has not occurred
No matter if I conquered, or was conquered

God's world is still the same, God's world is still good
The mountains still stand, trees still sway, rivers still flow
Spiders still spin webs

And when God turns the flashlight off
And I lie upon my bed at night
God whispers,
"I will be there again, in the morning,
Flashlight in hand."

The disciple in each of us is awakened slowly.
It is listening to love that awakens the disciple.

— Macrina Wiederkehr, OSB

My discipleship is quiet. I have at last realized that in spite of many missteps and mistaken directions, I have always enjoyed the Master's unqualified favor and always will, now and forever. Having heard at last the persistent voice of Love, I can now relax and be myself. I don't have to prove anything. I only have to follow the Master's lead. But it is my heart's desire to echo Love's song, to show everyone I meet that same loving regard, whether it is the harried check-out girl, the attendant in the parking garage, my secretary, or the custodian of my building. And, yes, the starving child in Darfur. I savor the truth of the poet W.H. Auden's words: "He [Jesus] is the Way. Follow Him through the Land of Unlikeness; You will see rare beasts and have unique adventures."

It is necessary…to fill myself with ideas that in the end lead my heart to the heart of the Divine. Then someday, somehow, the two hearts will beat in me as one.

— Joan Chittister

As we stand before life's problems, new tasks, or unfamiliar situations, dread may overwhelm us. In this gray space, our heart may feel very far from God's light and peace. We may feel as if we are lost in the wilderness, a long way from Eden.

But the choice is ours, now and always: to unite with the spirit of God, to share the space we are in. I find that reading a short devotion or meditation helps me to focus and realize that it is I who have moved and not God. My life is eased in direct proportion to my faith that God is there, in me and with me. My heart can beat with the heart of God, if I but take the time to listen.

Pay attention.
Be astonished.
Tell about it.

— Mary Oliver

I grew up in Florida where I spent my childhood closely watching the lizards; I noticed every detail on their tiny reptilian bodies. I looked at incredible birds and wildlife (not so incredible roaches) and I picked up shells, noticing the many details that made each one unique. I took time to appreciate the water and the way the light reflected off of it. I watched storms until I had to come in to safety. I was keenly aware of everything going on around me all the time. I paid attention. However, my teachers always wanted me to pay better attention in class. I spent and continue to spend a huge amount of energy trying to pay attention to the left brain details of my life, but what I love to do most is to pay attention to the world around me. The light reflecting off the water, raindrops on a leaf, many colored flowers, beautiful sunrises and sunsets, amazing creatures, and so much more. They all remind me that God is communicating love to each of us all the time.

Echoes of . . . Possibility

Dwell in possibility.

Thinking back on this week,
    What new possiblities did you consider?
    Were you able to be attuned to what's possible,
        while tuning out what's certain or wrong?
    How can you live into these new possibilities?

Pondering . . . Receptiveness

Most of us are better at giving than receiving.

How good are you at "receiving" from another?
What is God offering you that you are struggling to receive?
What prevents you from receiving what God wants to give you?

Be aware of your willingness to receive this week
...and gratefully count the gifts!

> *When we pray, how often do we say:"Speak, Lord, for your servant is listening?" More often, I think, we say:"Listen, Lord, for your servant is speaking!"*
>
> – Robert Wicks

The risers were filled with hundreds of middle school students waiting for their schedules on the first day of class. Who would their teachers be? Would they have friends in their classes? Would they have friends? First, they had to listen to the words I wanted to share to welcome them and guide them for the year ahead. It had to be brief to hold their attention. It had to be sincere and honest to hold their respect.

I told them I wanted to share a secret for success. "You have to listen," I told them. "You listen in three ways. First, you listen with your ears to take in what is being taught. Second, you listen with your mind, to make sense of what you hear. But the most important way you listen is with your heart. You listen with your heart when you choose to do those things that heal rather than hurt, forgive rather than hold a grudge, build rather than destroy, when you see and celebrate the Good in each person including yourself."

When we listen with our hearts to the Divine Presence, our prayer is "Show me the way I should go" rather than, "I want...," "I need...." It is in our heartfelt listening that we truly hear.

We spend so much of our adult energies thinking, planning, worrying, trying to get ahead or stay afloat, that we lose touch with that natural intimacy with God deep within us.

— C. Bourgeault

I am aware that I live too much in the future. This quote is a challenging reminder to me that I fail time and time again to live more fully in the present, where God is most accessible to me (and I to God). God is rarely present to me in the future because I crowd God out with worries, fears, or too many romantic dreams of my own selfish creation. I don't know why the future's uncertainty attracts me so, given the fact that it leads more often to anxiety rather than reassurance. It's a coping mechanism, I suppose—preparing for the worst, just in case. That leaves little room for faith however. Living in the present allows time to be fully available to God and everyone else in whom God is likewise present. How many missed opportunities for time with my family, or for conversations with friends, or for a moment of prayerful reflection have been missed in the present due to the distraction of the future?

Summer is a time to experience God in Sabbath moments, living in a "now" of rest and renewal rather than a "then" of unnecessary uncertainty.

And then there is that time to be, to simply be,
that time in which God quietly tells us who we
are and who God wants us to be.

— Madeline L'Engle

While wrestling with God some time ago about what I was to do or be, I heard a voice deep in my heart: "I want someone who will try. Try." So, being a good "do-bee," boy, did I try!! Praying, meditating, doing, doing, doing. Months later, though, I heard a gentler voice of that same God, changing my perspective on this directive.

When we encourage kids to try—playing a sport, writing for the school paper, or eating cauliflower—it's usually something different, something that implies risk. When God said "try," I too, was being asked to try something different: to try "to be," not to try "to do." "Trying to be" is a paradox; we can't try to be, we just BE! In our culture, "just being" is foreign, uncomfortable. Most of us don't even know where to begin.

In yoga, to open the stretch, you "soften" your muscles. This is different from other exercises—tensing muscles and pushing through the burn. In yoga, you can always stretch further when you soften. So too, when we "soften" our lives, allowing ourselves to just be, we open to the gentle voice of God, opening, stretching us, molding us into the gift we are—and are to be.

There is a candle in your heart, ready to be kindled.
There is a void in your soul, ready to be filled.
You feel it, don't you? . . .
Invite Him to fill you up, embrace the fire.

— Rumi

Candles are such wonderful tools. The simple light from one candle can illuminate an entire dark space. One small candle can't provide the same brightness of synthetic light, but the ambience of candle light can't be beat (though I must admit, a fire in the hearth on a cold night is stiff competition).

Easter begins with a single flame, the lighting of a Paschal fire from which a single candle bearing "the light of Christ" emerges from the tomb (traditionally a church graveyard) into our midst. The memory of Good Friday gives way to the first celebration of the Resurrection. Light breaks into the darkness, and the darkness is overcome.

So it is in our hearts when we allow Christ's simple and humble light to pierce the darkness of our souls. It doesn't take much light to vanquish that darkness, but we must be ready and willing for this Light to enter. This light is fueled by the oxygen of our humility and our willingness to recognize and acknowledge the void created by the darkness of our sin. The light of Christ brings warmth and the mysterious presence of the Holy Spirit. You feel it, don't you? Embrace the fire!

To listen is to lean in, softly, with a willingness to be changed by what we hear.

— Mark Nepo

Listening is often a lost skill in today's world. Our hurried, multitasked existence does not invite clear listening. Active listening is an essential ingredient in understanding and forming our most important relationships—it is central to loving others. We simply do not give others the gift of our undivided and careful attention.

Is there a relationship more important than our relationship with God? Are we not called to deepen that relationship by actively listening for God's voice? Today's quote calls to mind the phrase in the St. Francis prayer which reminds us to seek first "to understand rather than be understood."

Prayer is a time to seek to understand. When I communicate with God in prayer in a way which invites listening, my relationship deepens and grows. Praying simply for the knowledge of God's will for me and the strength to carry it out opens my heart and mind to hearing God's will for me. This challenges me to lean into my relationship, and to be open and willing to change. I can align my thoughts and actions with God's will as it is revealed to me—when I truly listen.

Echoes of . . . Receptiveness

Most of us are better at giving than receiving.

Thinking back on this week,
    Were you able to gratefully receive from another?
    Did you identify some things that cause you to struggle
       to receive?
    Were you aware of your willingness to receive this week?

Pondering . . . Silence

The sounds of silence surround us, if we only know how to hear them.

What are the places of silence in your life?
What do you hear if you are really silent?
What do you long to hear in the silence?

Listen to the sounds of silence this week.

> *Be still. Stop.*
> *There is no rush to get to the end,*
> *because we are never finished.*
>
> — Wayne Muller

The view from her window left her awestruck. Colors pale as pastel and rich as autumn intertwined intricately, bedazzling the young girl as she gazed at the meadow — God's garden — outside. How intently she could stare! How peaceful she felt when she did. Maybe if she collected a piece of every beautiful flower, leaf, and stone from it she would feel closer to God.

She immediately dashed outside, grabbing handfuls of flowers, leaves, and stones to drop by her window. Again and again, breathless but determined, she ran. Outside and inside, grabbing and dropping. After several trips, she leaned against her window panting. Bewildered, she wondered why all her hard work had not made her feel closer to God. In fact, she had felt closer when she had just sat gazing out at God's garden. Despite her hurried efforts, there was no way she could bring the majesty of the meadow inside. There was simply too much beauty to capture; she would never be able to grasp it all. She would find more contentment, more fulfillment by simply sitting and staring as she had been before.

And so, quietly and lovingly, she did.

Silence is the mother of truth.

— Benjamin Disraeli

I crave silence. I cherish solitude. I know that my wellbeing is rooted in silence, and yet I frequently get lost in the daily busyness and excuse myself from getting quiet. It's one of those heart/head things. My heart knows what I need to feel centered and whole, yet my head always has a to-do list screaming for attention. As silly as it sounds, I have started putting silence on my to-do list. This gives it priority and, at least for me, it works. Some days my silent time lasts longer and involves going outdoors for a walk, observing and listening to God's creation. Some days I squeeze in a few minutes sitting alone in the dark.

One of the blessings of the Well's recent pilgrimage to the Southwest was a day spent in silence in Chaco Canyon, NM. To walk where the ancients lived and to feel their presence in the vast quiet of that space filled my heart. A surprise moment of silence appeared in a busy hospital room. I held Isabella Rose, my new granddaughter, shortly after her birth and knew that she is my link to the future, just as the people of Chaco Canyon provide a link to the past. In both instances, the truth was clear: I am connected to all. How do you invite silence into your life? What places help you to open your spirit to a path of truth?

The purest faith has to be tested by silence
in which we listen for the unexpected, in which we are
open to what we do not yet know, and...gradually...
we will reach out to a new level of being with God.

— Thomas Merton

I first encountered the writings of Thomas Merton over 45 years ago when a friend gave me a copy of *Thoughts in Solitude*. I was familiar with solitude as a time of prayer and study, but this concept of solitude as a time of listening to God was new and exciting and more than a little unsettling.

Naturally, I found listening in solitude to be very difficult—I am so easily distracted! However, as time passed, it became somewhat easier. The sometimes surprising and always valuable insights I gained usually carried over into my life in my wider community. God sometimes places things directly in our hearts, but more often we find that God is speaking to us through others if we are listening. In my spiraling journey, I have often found God speaking to me through Merton's various writings.

Recently, I bought a new copy of *Thoughts in Solitude* to take on a retreat. My first copy is too tattered and worn to be used anymore, and the various other copies I have bought over the years have been given to friends who seemed to need them at that moment. I like to feel that we are all listening together.

I've come to realize that it's often in the most unlikely places that a sign appears, one that gives us just the message we need for our journey.

– Denise Roy

Michael Jackson's 1988 song "Man in the Mirror" had been swimming around in my mind for about a week, with the lyrics "If you want to make the world a better place, take a look at yourself, and then make a change" carving themselves into my subconscious bit by bit. I liked Jackson's sentiment because it closely paralleled my burgeoning understanding of inner peace, but I did not think much about the connection otherwise.

Later, at the Dodge Poetry Festival, Lucille Clifton quoted the very line from the song that had so touched me. Rather than believe that this occasion was purely coincidental, I chose to accept it as an encouragement—a sign that perhaps I was moving in the right direction. The reference made me feel connected to her; I took solace in the fact that someone else out there viewed inner peace in the same way I did. I was just becoming aware of my spiritual journey at this time, and Clifton's reference made it seem more real, more vitally important to me. Jackson understood it, Clifton understood it, and I was beginning to understand and feel it too. Signs of the spiritual life manifest themselves everywhere, but up until now I had not been ready to interpret and accept them, to incorporate them into my path.

Listen and look for God calling you . . .
God wants you to know God's purpose for you,
but the one God sends to you may be the least likely
person or come through unforeseeable circumstances.

— John E. Kitagawa

I've had enough encounters with "least likely" strangers to no longer be surprised by how God chooses to deliver his calling cards. "Unforeseeable circumstances" have also been regular teachers. What brought me up short recently however, was a nagging feeling I call "Holy Discontent." Now, discontent is not in my vocabulary. I long ago internalized expectations of a cheerful willingness to carry buckets made of stone whenever asked. But here was "Holy Discontent" — and it wasn't going away.

I had been asked to continue as Clerk of my Quaker Meeting. My normal ready answer of "yes" was replaced by "Holy Discontent." As I wrestled with this, things I normally did easily took more energy; things I looked forward to became dreaded tasks. I prayed to God about this change and received an answer: I was to say "yes, but": yes, I would serve, but only for one more year. Great blessings emerged from this "Holy Discontent." The community saw the need for clearer succession planning, and is working on the transition to a new clerk. Personally, I have been able to say "yes" to some new opportunities. I thought that carrying the same set of buckets made me faithful. I was sent the right inward teacher to learn that God wanted me to lay them down.

Echoes of . . . Silence

The sounds of silence surround us, if we only know how to hear them.

Thinking back on this week,
Recall any moments of true silence.
What did you hear when you were truly silent?
How did you listen for the unexpected?
How were you able to listen and look for God calling you?

Pondering . . . Truth

The sound of truth is not always easy to recognize.

In seeking truth, what do you listen for?
In what ways does truth emerge as you really listen?
How do you know when something is true?

This week, watch where truth emerges for you!

It has often occurred to me that a seeker of truth
has to be silent.

— Gandhi

Only the empty cup can be filled.

Cal was very sick, very disoriented. His speech was rambling,
sometimes incoherent. I knew that he had a history of emotional
breakdowns. We talked a little, prayed a little, and then both fell
silent. Cal seemed less agitated. I sat by the bed, comfortably
wordless.

After perhaps half an hour, gradually Cal began talking, making
perfect sense, and I realized that he was making a confession, though
he himself might not have called it that. "Wait, Cal," I said, "you are
seeking reconciliation and I should be wearing my purple stole." I took
the stole from my hospital-call case and put it on.

"Oh," he said, "may I touch it, may I hold it?" "Of course," I said.
"Please do." He gripped one end of the stole tightly, stroking its gold
embroidered cross with his other hand. He was silent again for a long
time, focused on the stole, and then the story began to flow. When it
ended, I was able to say, "Cal, God has forgiven your sins." Then the
tears also flowed.

Sell your cleverness and buy bewilderment.

— Rumi

What is to be said about a society or culture that reveres the clever-minded as opposed to those who embrace creative thought? Is it that those who, by their own will, appear to have gained control over their lives, thus giving the impression that the uncertainties and vagaries of life have been mastered?

Individuals, societies, cultures, and civilizations achieve great heights resulting from the intelligent will of purposeful people. Such persons seek to gain control over their lives, and in many instances, the lives of others.

Time passes, the cycle is repeated, and the illusion of control inevitably succumbs to the inherent flow of life. Control and certainty erode, leaving clever minded people fearful and asking "How did this happen?" and in extreme circumstances, "Who can we blame?" At those moments of questioning, step back and look to see what has remained constant. Look to see what survives. It is a person's assimilation into the depths of creativity, be it their own or that of someone else's creative endeavor.

What is the source of such imaginings? What is the source of these surviving expressions? The sublime wonder of it all!

Perhaps wisdom lies not in the constant struggle to bring the sacred into daily life but in the recognition that . . . we are always on sacred ground.

— Rachel Naomi Remen

I recently experienced (almost simultaneously) two very opposite extremes of the gift of life, which I now recognize as moments of existing or being on "sacred ground".

The birth of my grand nephew has brought a breath of life and awe into my life and the lives of my family members. The smiles and delights of this pre-toddler discovering how to stand, clap, and squeal with joy have filled our hearts with love and gratitude as we witness this wonderful miracle.

At almost the same time, we have also watched sadly the gradual diminishment of our dear mother who was blessed with ninety-eight years of a life filled with total love and dedication to her family. It was a gift to be in the presence of an older prayerful woman who cherished every moment she had to live, love, and laugh. Along with that came the love, support, and strength received from family and friends when a loved one goes home to God.

Truly, the sacred is part of our daily lives if we just pause long enough to recognize it. We are indeed standing on Holy Ground every day.

In searching for the truth, be ready for the unexpected.

— Heraklietos of Ephesos

Some of us are more comfortable operating under the assumption that we have control over most of our life. We choose whether or not to pay attention to our rousing morning alarm, to begin our day with coffee and something to nourish our bodies, to take that morning walk or run, and sail on to work or play. For the big decisions we may consult our friends or family, ponder over that list of pros and cons, ultimately taking the road that seems most sensible, given all the information we have at the moment.

I wonder why it is that only after wrestling unsuccessfully with a decision on my own, when I am most desperately seeking guidance, that I remember there is, after all, another approach. What if I were to let go of the decision altogether and hand it right over to the Wise One? God will point me toward the truth. It may be a surprising gift, a third option that I had never considered, or one that may not seem so "sensible" at that moment. The next step may be the hardest and yet the most freeing—to take that choice that God hands us and run with it.

Let your life speak.
Before you tell your life what you intend to do with it,
listen for what it intends to do with you.

— Parker Palmer

Any artist can describe how frustrating it feels to "force" a work of art. Particularly when the gallery opening is just a week away, or the recital is right around the corner, or the order for the handmade stationery must be filled. Who knows what it might be that presses us into creating, but it is not a good feeling. Sure, the product happens, but the process has somehow been unsettled. Any artist will tell you that art isn't made; art emerges. A block of stone becomes a sculpture through a process of the artist relating to the medium in an intimate and thoughtful way. A painting becomes vivid and meaningful only when the painter decides to let the colors speak to her. As creations ourselves, we are no different. There is a voice inside of us, wanting to emerge, wanting to be heard. Listen, knowing that the true you, the work-of-art you, the divine-creation you, will emerge.

Echoes of . . . Truth

The sound of truth is not always easy to recognize.

Thinking back on this week,
    As you listened, in what ways did truth emerge?
    Were there any surprises? What sounds or feelings
        were evoked by truth?
    What truths emerged for you?

Pondering . . . Courage

Courage is a movement in the heart.
("Cour" in French means heart)

To what is your heart calling you?
What feelings surface as you ponder your heart's call?
Where are courage, risk, and daring emerging in you?

> *Trust in yourself. Your perceptions are often far*
> *more accurate than you are willing to believe.*
>
> — Claudia Black

"Keep your eye on Jesus," Linda told me.

I was venting about a problem with a friend—I just wanted this person out of my life. Linda insisted that I not give up, that I pray about it and confront this friend. "Put your trust in God," Linda advised. "Then you will be able to trust in yourself." I took her advice. Trusting in God allowed me to overcome my fear of confrontation and resolve the problem. We tend to avoid confrontation, taking what seems to be the easiest but not necessarily the right path. We avoid problems, staying in a safe place within social norms. It is a less stressful and time-consuming approach. Taking time to pray for guidance does not fit our hectic schedules.

When we do pray the outcome is better, not always in the short term, but most certainly in the long term. Trusting God gave me strength and I knew I had done the right thing. Not trusting in God brings self doubt and confusion. Trusting God brings self confidence and peace. We can trust ourselves and our perceptions because we are walking with God. As Linda knew "keeping my eye on Jesus" was the only path to take. Great advice I will never forget.

> *We must be willing to get rid of the life we've planned,*
> *so as to have the life that is waiting for us.*
>
> — Joseph Campbell

I never planned my life's big decisions: career, marriage, where I would live—things just happened almost in spite of myself. As a teenager, I loved to read so I thought that I might become a librarian. In college, I began as an English major but within two years, I had changed to Philosophy. On a whim, I went to law school. That was over 25 years ago—who knew?

I married a nice young man with a similar background and settled near our parents. Within ten years, I was divorced and had moved to a different state—who knew? I never planned to have children. Ten years later, I have two wonderful children with my second husband— who knew? Well, perhaps God knew.

These decisions were not planned but have led me to a wholly unexpected and very happy life. My leaps into the unknown and unplanned have taken me places that I never expected. And even though I now live a settled life, I know it could change. I suspect that many of us lead lives like this. We trust God and our instincts to lead us. Hopefully, we can then look at our lives and be happy with what God has given us even though the people and events are ones that we never could have planned.

All serious daring starts from within.

– Eudora Welty

Dictionaries conclude that there is an element of courage in daring acts. I agree. Whenever I leave my comfort zone to step out and express my inner self, I am exposed to the possibility of consequences I may not want. It is a risky decision to make. Am I willing to deal with the consequences, whatever they may be, in order to give my inner self a voice?

In the process of making serious daring decisions, I need the wisdom of a loving God to direct me and give me the tools of discernment. I believe the seeds of daring thoughts are scattered around us all the time. Some are subtle and slow to germinate; others are urgent and aggressive. The willingness of my heart to be a listening heart that invites God to guide me seems to determine where, when, and how I allow the seeds of daring to enter my thoughts and take root.

I am reminded of the Parable of the Sower (Matthew 13:1-23). The seed that thrives is the one that fell on soil belonging to a person with a fertile mind: one whose ears not only hear but who also understands.

The movement of the Spirit of God in the hearts of people often calls them to act...they are given to wisdom and courage to dare a deed that challenges and to kindle a hope that inspires.

— Howard Thurman

The prophets of Hebrew Scripture were rarely the most popular folks, not always the most well—liked. No prophet, for that matter, is universally likeable. The words of the prophet are often harsh, speaking clarity in situations and amidst circumstances that often are not ready for clarity.

Yet, the Spirit of God moves in just that way. The Spirit moves in a way that often brings uneasiness, not comfort. A priest in the parish where I grew up once said that the pit in your stomach that says, "No. This isn't right," is the Holy Spirit working. This is the moment when we are given the opportunity to live out the wisdom and courage that Thurman speaks about. It is in these moments, when we respond to and speak to some inner and divine truth, that we are living out the Spirit of God.

I don't know of a prophet who thought her life was easy, who couldn't wait to deliver messages from God. I do know that the world changes —the kingdom comes—when we speak to that discomfort— the Spirit of God.

Any ordinary favor we do for someone
or any compassionate reaching out may seem
to be going nowhere at first, but may be
planting a seed we can't see right now.
— Sharon Salzberg

I believe there is a master plan, and we are all a part of this ever-growing plan—this woven tapestry of circumstances. I also believe that God is in all of our circumstances.

Each day we come in contact with others, sometimes only for a moment, but I believe we are meant, at that very time, to be connected. Each connection is an opportunity to plant a seed—or not. It is my choice, God's gift of free will. The purpose is to plant the seeds of love, kindness, and compassion in the world - to give, not to take.

There are no coincidences, but rather a master plan that only the Almighty can control. It is up to me to surrender and follow my heart. It is only then that I can listen and hear what God is telling me, for God is found within my heart. To trust is to have faith, to have faith is to surrender, and to surrender means God is in control, not me.

Echoes of . . . Courage

Courage is a movement in the heart.
("Cour" in French means heart)

Thinking back on this week,
    To what did your heart call you?
    Where did courage, risk, and daring emerge in you?
    How did you respond to the movement of the Spirit of God?

Pondering . . . The Inner Voice

The Inner Voice longs to be heard.

How can you become more aware of your Inner Voice?
How do you recognize your Inner Voice and befriend it?
In what ways do you ignore, overlook, or even reject your Inner Voice?

This week, celebrate stillness!

If we can locate, at the center of our existence,
our individual 'still, small voice,' we will have found
our greatest ally in life.

— Robert Lawrence Smith

My first reaction to this quote is a whimsical one—the image of Horton from Dr. Seuss pops into my head. Thinking a little deeper, I remember those times that a "still, small voice" has urged me to act, or prevented me from acting or over-reacting. I often wonder, "Whose voice am I hearing?" An angel? A guardian angel, perhaps? I like to think so. We think about angels as being somewhere outside ourselves, but are they really at the center of our existence? And where is that, exactly? Was the story of Horton, the gentle elephant who heard a small voice and acted to save an infinitesimal world that he couldn't see, a metaphor for faith?

July 21

All things in the universe want to be heard,
as do the many voices inside us.

— Frederick and Mary Ann Brussat

Yikes! Now I have to confess...there are many voices inside that awaken me in the middle of the night with their incessant chatter. The "worrier" is the loudest voice droning on and on about the same thing like a hamster going round and round on a wheel. Sometimes, the only way I can silence the voices is to get up and write. By doing this, I make room in my head and heart for the voice I need most in my life... the voice of God.

God's voice, for me, is not loud and booming. Instead, it is often a nudge or a still, small voice within that prompts me to pray for someone, mend a hurt, or write a letter that, unknown to me, was just what someone needed. When I clear the way and make time for silence and prayer, I can better hear God's voice—a voice that never steers me wrong.

Listen! Something strains to be born, to shake itself free;
something brand new trembles at the far edge of our
minds: the shape of a world to come conceived
in our present labor and pain.

— Catherine de Vinck

Listen! As I read that word, it resonates. Training in listening ministries has taught me the power of Spirit-led listening to others. However, Catherine de Vinck asks me to walk what is often a more difficult path, listening to what is deep inside my own heart.

Listen! I wait and walk and watch with wonder as the seasons cycle through the year. What is God telling me when the pale halo of green appears on grey trees? Something new is beginning. Listen! God reminds me that God is in charge, and my job is to hear the soft voice—reminding me to be patient, to wait, for change evolves in God's time, kairos time. The evolution excites me. I continue to dream through the process as the pale early greens turn darker, as they shade me through the summer. The brilliant colors of the autumn accompany me as I grow. It is a rich season of harvest, a time to reflect on how I have listened and how God has led. When the trees turn grey again, I can rest a bit, knowing that in this never-ending cycle, there will always be something new straining to be born.

*The inner voices of the body want to speak to us,
to inform us of the truths beneath the fixed surface
of our external lives.*

— John O'Donohue

Wisdom

I always thought that it was me
That flowed and drenched and touched the lips
And time and people, luck and chance
Were falls and dams and rocks and dips

Each day I woke there was the hope
That I could quench the thirsty need
That I could soothe the sunburned heart
That I could fill, that I could feed

But passing days unearthed the truth
These lofty thoughts were just a dream
At best I helped the river bend
But mostly I just blocked the stream

For I just never understood
It took me years to ever see
That I was but the river's bed
The current flowing over me

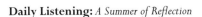

There is a voice inside of you, That whispers all day long,
'I feel that this is right for me, I know that this is wrong.'
No teacher, preacher, parent, friend, Or wise man can decide
What's right for you - just listen to
The voice that speaks inside.

— Shel Silverstein

There is a deep Voice...a Voice ready to bathe us with unspeakable love...a Voice that knows the depths of who we are. This Voice speaks our name gently...lovingly. It is this Voice we want to echo through our souls. This Voice constantly invites us into conversation.

Yet, even when we are aware of and hear God's Voice...we have trouble listening. What if the message God speaks does not match our expectations? Will it justify our comfortable lives? Will we question that it is really God's Voice? Maybe we are just hearing things. Maybe fear drowns out the Voice as God calls us to be still and to listen. Maybe self-doubt muffles the sweet sound that speaks our worth.

Here is the Good News—the One who loves us best will pursue us with whispers, with poetry and music, through friends and loved ones, through spoken and written word, through silence and the beauty of creation. God will wait...loving us...never letting us go...constantly speaking our name—until we turn our face toward the Light. When we open our inward ears, and when conversation takes place through Truth, Spirit blooms. We know Love completely—we are known completely.

Echoes of . . . the Inner Voice

The Inner Voice longs to be heard.

Thinking back on this week,
In what ways were you aware of your Inner Voice?
What does your Inner Voice sound like?
How were you able to befriend your Inner Voice?

Pondering . . . Opportunity

Opportunity knocks, and we need to listen in order to open the door.

In what ways do the unexpected and the difficult offer you a gift?
What does opportunity's knocking sound like? Is it a loud banging or
a soft tapping?
Who or what helps you to open the door to opportunity?

Be attentive this week to the surprises hidden in your problems!
What doors will you open?

We are often blessed in ways we can't imagine.
Instead of getting what we want, we get what we need.
The problem is that it takes longer to understand
that what we didn't want is precisely what,
in the end, was best for us . . . .

— Joan Chittister

High on a lakeside bluff, in the Eastern Townships of Quebec, sits a rustic, seasonal cabin that has been in my husband's family for more than 100 years. It was here, in 1977, that he courted me during cloudless, sky-blue days that seemed never to end. I have spent almost every summer since in this tiny corner of Canada, carrying dreams of it in my heart on dark winter days.

My most recent stay was in stark contrast to the first blissful summer more than thirty years ago. Recently retired, I yearned for days in a hammock, endless tennis games, picnics on our stony beach, long walks, and moonlit canoe rides. Instead we were besieged with torrential rains, flooded shores, and record-breaking disappointment. As one wet day begat another, I struggled to know what to do with myself. Being still and quiet doesn't come easy.

Yet the daily sound of rain on the roof led me slowly to a place of quiet reflection where God was waiting for me. Forced to go at a different pace, I let my soul rest in ways a more active summer wouldn't have provided. And now, months later, from a season I didn't want, I carry memories of a soggy summer full of blessings and grace.

The truth is that our finest moments are most likely to occur when we are feeling deeply uncomfortable, unhappy, or unfulfilled.

— M. Scott Peck

"You are probably not in enough pain to make the change you want to make." I have actually been bold enough to say this to people who came to me for counsel or advice. People are shocked by this statement, because they are already facing great emotional and spiritual anguish.

It takes great compassion to address another's pain, and great patience to address our own. If I have learned to be compassionate with myself, then I will have a greater chance of being compassionate with another. When Scripture exhorts us to be compassionate as God is compassionate, it is not just referring to others. Most of our compassionate learning stems from the pain of life we have experienced.

I know a woman from Rwanda who has forgiven those who killed her family members. She was in great anguish and distress for a long time. She realized in being compassionate towards herself that forgiveness was her only way back into life. Facing the greatness of her pain allowed her to take this step. So she forgave.

God sometimes seems to speak to us most intimately
when God catches us, as it were, off our guard.

– C.S. Lewis

I am perhaps most "off my guard" while relaxing, listening to music. I often hear God speaking to me through songs on my car radio or on my iPod. And since I don't listen to "Christian" stations, some people are surprised that I hear God in secular music. Yet I have learned about forgiveness from Don Henley, a Christian response to "street people" from Nanci Griffith, and the meaning of freedom from Kris Kristofferson.

From my perspective, these musical heralds are not that different from the unlikely messengers whom God sometimes chose to deliver God's Word, like Rahab the prostitute or Zacchaeus the tax collector. What I have learned is to listen with an open mind, ready to receive God at anytime.

In the middle of difficulty lies opportunity.

— Albert Einstein

When I look back and listen to my life, I realize that the most challenging periods have been doorways to important discoveries about myself, God, others, and all of life.

One particular crisis, involving a broken relationship, left me heartbroken and shaken to my core. I sat in my deep sadness and pleaded with God to show me how I could live without this person. As I listened for God's response, I became aware of little glimmers of light that God was offering me through friends, nature, and my daily encounters in life. It was amazing. If I really looked and listened carefully, I could see God trying to guide me to healing and wholeness. It took time, but gradually, I found new, healthier ways of living without this relationship.

I am grateful for our God who lovingly accompanies us in our difficulties, providing enough light for the next step, and making all things new. We just need to remember to watch for the light.

Everything that happens to you has the potential to deepen you. It brings to birth within you new territories of the heart.

— John O'Donohue

Everything that happens has the potential to deepen us, but that deepening does not automatically occur. It almost certainly does not occur without some work and risk on our part. When things happen in our lives, it is usually far easier to stay on the superficial side of them, not letting them get to us. Yet, some things should get to us! Some events are meant to encourage us to do the work of pondering their meanings.

Pondering does not mean that we obsess over things, but that we find the pearl in the unattractive shell, the diamond in the rough. And that involves a risk. Maybe we won't find the pearl we expected or the diamond for which we hoped. Maybe we won't give birth to the dream we had envisioned.

We often flee from risk because we want to protect ourselves from disappointment. Too bad—our fearfulness means that we rarely entertain the thought that the risk might bring to life a better, more authentic reality than we could have ever dared to imagine.

August 1

Echoes of . . . Opportunity

Opportunity knocks, and we need to listen in order to open the door.

Thinking back on this week,
In what ways did the unexpected and the difficult offer you
a gift?
What surprises were hidden in your problems?
What doors opened for you?

August 2

Pondering . . . Listening to Each Other

Listening is the greatest gift we can offer another.

Who listens to your heart?
To whom and with whom do you listen?
What do you experience when someone truly listens to you?

Be grateful this week for the Holy Listeners in your life.

One of the easiest human acts is also the most healing.
Listening to someone. Simply listening. Not advising or
coaching, but silently and fully listening.

— Margaret Wheatley

There is a TV ad for Rice Krispies, where the mom tells the child to "listen hard." I have been thinking about that phrase, "listen hard." We use it when the thing to be heard is faint or distant—like "snap, crackle, and pop," or serious—like instructions or scolding.

It occurs to me that when I "listen hard," I have a tendency to listen with my head (often, my very hard head!), thinking about what advice to give or what interesting, clever, or consoling thing to say in response. My best listening, though, is when I "listen soft," when I listen with my heart. When I "listen soft," the words shared by the other find a warm place to rest. They sink deeply into my core, so that any word uttered in response is a real and true reflection of the other's experience. They know they have been heard.

Today, try to feel, rather than to fix; to soothe, rather than to solve. "Listen soft." Listen with your heart.

Listening is a magnetic and strange thing, a creative force.

— Karl Menninger

Do you remember Sister Mary Clarence and the choir of nuns singing, "My Guy" in the movie "Sister Act"? When I listen to the nuns singing these words:

> Nothing you can say can tear me away from my guy.
> Nothing you could do, cause I'm stuck like glue, to my guy.
> I'm sticking to my guy, like a stamp to a letter,
> like birds of a feather, we stick together.
> I can tell you from the start, I can't be torn apart from my guy.
> Nothing you could do, could make me be untrue, to my guy.
> (lyrics by Smokey Robinson)

I envision the parishioners pondering these questions:
Can we see God as their "My Guy"? Does a creator God pull us in?
How strong is this force? What does God's voice sound like? How can we enrich the world when we listen?

How do you ponder these questions?

> *The greatest benefit of listening is that it moves us closer*
> *to one another.*
>
> — Margaret Wheatley

If I am actively and truly listening to someone else, I set aside my own thoughts and agendas and devote my entire attention to the other. I listen not only to the words that person is saying, but to the tone, to the emotion conveyed, and to nonverbal clues, so that I can comprehend both the words and the feelings. However momentary this setting aside of myself may be, it allows the possibility of seeing that person more clearly, understanding that person more deeply, and of being open to what God may be saying to me through this person.

When a person listens to me and gives that same deep attention, I sometimes feel I have exposed some portion of myself that is perhaps not apparent in normal everyday conversation. It is our knowledge of each other and this willingness to be mutually vulnerable that builds intimacy and draws us closer. As we draw closer to each other, we are building a connection. As we each extend connections to others, we are building community.

For listening is the act of entering the skin of the other
and wearing it for a time as if it were our own.

— David Spangler

It is hard to be a good listener. Being a good listener requires that we do our best to focus all of our attention on the person who is speaking. This can be difficult when the speaker takes a long time to get to the point, or when we are distracted by exterior noise, which in our culture is both substantial and ubiquitous.

More importantly, we are often distracted by the interior noise of our own thoughts and judgments, which can be deafening. This divides our attention and makes it impossible to be fully present to the person who is speaking. And being fully present is what it means to be in another's skin. After all, how much more present can we be to someone than to be in his or her skin? And when we are in another's skin, we become a part of him or her, and he or she surely becomes a part of us. Indeed, true listening requires that we become part of the person speaking, if even for just a few moments, so that we see a situation from his or her perspective, as much as if we were seeing with his or her own eyes.

> *They say that spirits make music by moving through*
> *the breaks in what is living. If so, the work of love*
> *is to hold each other and listen.*
>
> — Mark Nepo

This poetic expression suggests that spiritual music is often made from the shattered fragments of our lives—our mishaps and stumbling, our suffering. For me, "music" implies at least the potential for harmony with some deeper or truer strain. To recognize the music of our pain is to become reconciled to it, to accept it when it cannot be avoided, and, if possible, to learn from it. Listening to this music invites resonance with a greater good or knowledge, if indeed our suffering is to be redeemed.

But what is this work of "holding" and "being held?" Why do we need that? Why do we need to give and receive that? Because love is never solitary; love implies the duality of a lover and the beloved. So the act of love is the expression of unity—of oneness of consciousness— in this dualistic world. When we hold someone in love, we affirm our ultimate identity with them and with the Spirit within. We hold each other and listen not to effect our healing or assuage our wounds, but to embrace together our common ground. Perhaps it is "to blow the dust from each other's eyes," which, according to an African proverb, is the reason two antelopes walk together. So it is that salvation can be found in community.

Echoes of . . . Listening to Each Other

Listening is the greatest gift we can offer another.

Thinking back on this week,
> Who were those who listened to your heart?
> How did you experience listening as life-giving?
> What gifts did you discover as you listened to others? As
> others listened to you?

Pondering . . . Paying Attention

We miss so much in life because we are focused elsewhere.

What does it mean to really pay attention?
What helps you to pay attention?
What blessings have you known simply because you were paying
attention at the right moment?

Let your ponderings this week heighten your awareness!

This is the first, wildest, and wisest thing I know,
that the soul exists, and that it is built entirely
out of attention.

— Mary Oliver

Our soul is our self, our essence, the purest reflection of who we are. The soul is built by attention, yes, but on the foundation of our life's experiences and, more importantly, on our relationships. Reflection (attention, meditation, prayer) allows us to consider these experiences and relationships from other points of view. Reflection mellows and intensifies, soothes and pains, intensifies and numbs—it hones our experiences and perfects our relationships. This reflection is our conversation with God about ourselves—it is how we interact with God, how we receive God's feedback, and how we ultimately end up being who we really are.

If we pay attention to our soul through our conversations with ourselves and with God, our soul becomes more aware, enlightened, and interesting. For me, it also becomes a little more open-minded—allowing for more possibilities in experiences, in relationships, and with God.

Listening is a . . . kind of striving not to strive,
for self-striving would make noise and prevent us
from hearing...

— Beatrice Bruteau

On a recent retreat, the leader made the startling statement that achievement of any goal is dangerous on the spiritual journey. This can be easily understood as a restatement of the old adage that we learn more from our failures than from our successes. But the danger of paying attention to achievements is that we become rewarded by the world's reaction to them, that we begin to equate success in our lives with achieving. The striving which can result stirs up a lot of dust and noise which can obscure the Way ahead.

Learning to do God's work in the world without striving for success is one of the greatest challenges of the spiritual life. Striving and listening are competing for the same space. When we are listening whole-heartedly, there is no room for striving and vice versa. Listening is indispensable to living the life that God intends for us, and to achieving the authentic success of allowing God's purpose to flow through our lives.

Silence is God's gift to our minds, a gift that modern life seems to have lost or crowded out.

— Robert Lawrence Smith

I do not function well without silence.

This is a lesson I learned early as a young mother. While my infant son would nap, I'd catch up on chores. But invariably he would awaken refreshed and I would be frazzled and sometimes resentful. My head was spinning: I wanted to be the perfect wife and mother, but the work seemed overwhelming. "How do other mothers do this?" I cried to myself as I flopped into a large arm chair.

As I sat, the stress melted away, and I pondered the reality of my situation: as long as I have a baby, I'll never catch up. Almost in tears, I prayed a small prayer, "God, I'm tired, help me deal with this." Soon a sense of peace and silence relaxed me, and when my son awoke, I felt fresh and ready to be a mom again. Remembering that sense of peace and silence, the next day I closed my eyes to the laundry basket filled with baby clothes and eagerly returned to that same chair, wondering if the quiet and peace would return. It did. And thus began a practice that I continue to this day, regardless of where I am in life. And when I do, I always return to the world a quieter self.

Let your words be few.

— Ecclesiastes 5:2 (NIV)

Are we not told in our Christian faith to go out and bring the good news of the kingdom of God to all that would hear? How can that be done with few words? According to Arthur Hinds, author of *The Complete Sayings of Jesus Christ*, the number of words in the New Testament is 181,253, with barely over only 20 percent being the words of Christ. But, oh! Such mighty words.

When I received this quote "Let your words be few" as my assignment for the reflection book, I thought of the word LISTEN! It is amazing how just our listening can be helpful or comforting to those in joy or distress—but only if we listen with our full attention. We can honor the spirit within others by listening to their feelings, their joys, their sorrows, their news, and their stories, as we allow our own words to be few. A simple greeting, a hug, smile, or a sympathetic tear or ear, reflect one's caring and concern without the spoken word.

One of my favorite quotations, attributed to St. Francis of Assisi, is "Preach the Gospel at all times. If necessary, use words."

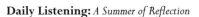

God often speaks in whispers.

— Joyce Rupp

If that is the case, then I am in big trouble. I don't hear whispers. I hear digital surround-sound, car-beeping, kid-singing, referee-whistling, voice-mail beeping, fax-screeching, in-your-face sounds all day long. If that is the case, then I'm missing a piece of divine communication. That could be serious and unknown, like a missed cell phone call. What if it is really important? What if God wants me to bring the tablets down the mountain? Part the Chesapeake Bay? Cure cancer? Debate Sarah Palin? Bring snacks to Saturday's soccer game?

If that is the case, then I'm confused. God knows that he can't speak to me in whispers. What we, God and I, have discovered, in my non-fat, grande latte haze, is that God speaks to me through WYPR. I'm not joking. God knows me. I have asked God for direction and asked specifically that it not be in the form of a chrysalis ten feet high in a sycamore tree in the far corner of our yard or in obscure cloud formations between the hours of 5:00 and 6:00 am. No, God knows that I need a bull-horn and not hushed tones. If that is the case, then I might have to change my behavior. I might have to…"Hold on, God. You'll have to speak up. The phone is ringing…"

Echoes of . . . Paying Attention

_____

We miss so much in life because we are focused elsewhere.

Thinking back on this week,
  How did you experience "paying attention" in a new way?
  What blessings did you discover simply because you were
    paying attention at the right moment?
  How did paying attention affect the rest of your life?

August 16

Pondering . . . Adventure

_____

Life is an adventure, new every moment!

What would it look like for you to approach each day as an adventure?
How might God be calling you to adventure in your daily life?
How do the unexpected, exciting parts of life offer you wisdom?

This week, listen for exciting, unexpected invitations into adventure
with God!

*Accept the wisdom of your soul. Listen to the words
it speaks. Observe the visions and dreams it creates,
and respond to your soulful feelings.*

— Bernie S. Siegel

How does the soul speak?

With a yearning...with a cry...with a strong surge of emotion. When I
know with my inner knowing that something is right...or that something is wrong.

The soul speaks through the body's sensations that say, "Breathe and
stay with this;" or, "Let yourself into this moment of love and wonder."

When I am open and listening, the soul speaks in a sound that flows
up from deep inside and enters with a press through the pores of my
skin. And then sometimes, I weep with gratitude for the message, for
the ability to yield, for the felt presence of wise benevolence around
me, around us.

The wisdom of the soul is our deep and constant pull towards one
another. The soul draws us into relationship with all souls, into a oneness with all things living. Thank God that the soul is blind to political
constructions, to the color of skin, to material wealth. The soft gaze of
the soul sees the truth, which is our goodness, in each of us.

Trust that still, small voice that says,
"This might work and I'll try it."

— Diane Mariechild

Why not try it? What's really at stake here?

That still, small voice comes from somewhere within, and its message contains at least some small degree of wisdom, credibility, or creativity. I don't need to justify the outcome in the beginning stage. I just need to know I am coming from the right place within, and that I am willing to give my best effort to deal with a problem. I don't have to be a superhero.

I remember years ago when I was learning the steps of the scientific method. It never began with an outcome, only a thoughtful question based on an observation. The whole process was a series of steps that led to either a conclusion answering the question, or not. Often it led to other questions and more tests. It is an "I'll try it" process.

It's easy to forget that the whole world does not dangle on my successes or failures. My part is just a step, an attitude, a spirit that may lead to something bigger and has greater significance than I have by myself. I need to trust that still, small voice and move on.

We cannot escape fear. We can only transform it into a companion that accompanies us on all our exciting adventures . . . Take a risk a day.

— Susan Jeffers

Fear and dread hover over us on occasion, but they need not define our days or our lives. We can recognize their presence as part of our whole, but not all of it. If we humbly ask the Holy Spirit to accompany us and guide us, we can step out in faith, whether it is to a new job, a new relationship, or a new activity.

Avoiding fear and risk gets us stuck in our comfort zone, a place where we cannot develop and live life to the fullest. I am confident that living colorless, drab lives in quiet desperation is not God's plan for his creation.

Spiritual training is a lot like physical training—the more we exercise the stronger we become. Remember the Nike slogan, "Just do it"? As we take that risky step, others will sense in us the power of God's grace at work in human life. What greater accomplishment can we achieve?

You have to trust the inner voice that shows the way...
Only by attending constantly to the inner voice can you be
converted to a new life of freedom and joy.

— Henri J.M. Nouwen

I love helping others, but oh how I struggle with giving others the op-portunity to do something for me. I don't like being beholden, and yet, what a blessing it is to allow others the joy of giving. Then one day I listened to the eyes of a child.

The furnace in my apartment had broken on a particularly cold day. I decided this was an ideal time to go to the warm laundromat to do my wash. I stopped in the convenience store next door to get some cof-fee. A father and small son were at the coffee counter when I arrived. We greeted each other and commiserated about the cold weather. I shared that I was without heat and hoped it would be repaired soon.

The gentleman proceeded to check-out and I finished pouring my coffee. When I got in line, the man said to the cashier that he would also pay for my coffee. Just as I was going to say, "No, thank you," I glimpsed into the eyes of the child looking up at his father with such pride at his father's kindness, that I stopped, and smiling instead said, "Thank you." It took the eyes of a child for me to stop and listen to that still small voice in each of us.

*Have the courage to begin the new life that each day
brings you.*

— Bernie S. Siegel

Birth, marriage, divorce, death, reversal of financial health, chronic
illness, or limitation...all of these are life events in which, one
moment, we are familiar with our routine, we know how to function,
we know the rules, we know the dance...and in the next moment
we do not.

It is through such experiences that I have come to know the truth that
the only constant in all that comes our way is God's love and faith-
fulness. As I humbly release my need for schedules, planning, and
control, I melt into the loving arms of God, who is ever ready to gently
accompany and guide me along the next step in the path of life.

When I am weak, confused, lonely, or afraid, I gain strength by trusting in the loving presence of God. What gives me courage in the face
of fear and the unknown is the truth that I do not walk alone.

August 22

Echoes of . . . Adventure

Life is an adventure, new every moment!

Thinking back on this week,
    How did a spirit of adventure affect your week?
    How were you invited into adventure?
    What adventurous parts of your life offered you wisdom?

August 23

Pondering . . . Wonder

Children can teach us how to live in wide-eyed wonder.

What are some of your memories of experiencing wonder and delight?
What are those things that fill you with wonder and delight?
What would your life look like if you lived in wide-eyed wonder?

Listen to a little child this week...or to your own inner child.
May you be led into wonder!

Don't underestimate the value of doing nothing,
of just going along, listening . . .

—A. A. Milne

The word that leaps out at me as I reflected on this quote is
PRESENCE. Think about what it means when a friend or someone
whom we might not even know very well is just there in the darkness
or the pain of a loss, a crisis, a disappointment, or any hard time.
Words are often not what makes something better. Instead, it is having someone there, even in the silence, that makes all the difference.

People often become concerned about knowing the right words to say
when someone has died or when visiting a hospital, nursing home,
detention center, jail, etc. The simple fact that we are there—to listen,
support, or just be present– that's more important than the words we
utter.

Sometimes, we view this being present as doing nothing, just going
along. But a listening heart, and the desire just to be present to the
other, is often the only thing wanted or needed. Presence, listening,
just being there, holds a value that cannot be underestimated
because it is a gift—and a mutual one at that!

Each day comes bearing its own gifts.
Untie the ribbons.

— Mary Oliver

Every day is a gift. As someone who has been diagnosed with a terminal illness, I have discovered a new appreciation for every new day. Sometimes, it is tempting to allow myself to give in to the warmth and comfort of my bed and sleep for awhile longer. Now, though, I have a new awareness of time running out, and I realize that waking is not endless. I need to get up and be certain to fully experience the joys that await every day that I can.

Before, I thought of everything differently—like it was a count down. "Ah, if today is a waste, then surely I am closer to tomorrow, and that will be much better."

Not so anymore. Now I see a finite number of days, perhaps enough to fit under a Christmas tree and each may be opened to see the treasure within. But I have to get up Christmas morning, and every morning, to see the gifts. Merely looking at them is not enough. First we admire the beauty of the gift of the day, slowly savoring the ribbons as we pull them off, and then open the lovely treasure inside, with true thanksgiving for each and every one.

The most beautiful thing we can experience is the mysterious.

— Albert Einstein

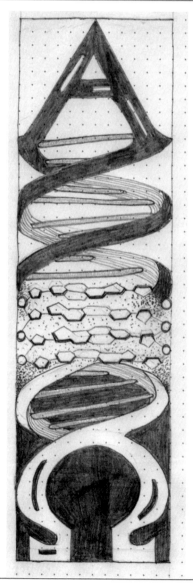

People travel to wonder at the height of the mountains, at the huge waves of the seas…at the vast compass of the ocean, at the circular motion of the stars, and yet they pass by themselves without wondering. —Augustine

Several years have passed since I stood on the beach gazing at the ocean. I have always been mesmerized by the ocean's sheer magnitude and power, its richness as a source of life sustaining treasures, and beyond all else, its drama and beauty as it creates spiking images of waves and sounds of frothy percussion. On this particular day my thoughts were drawn to my own finite existence…so remote from the infinite status of the ocean. Momentarily, selfish childhood longings to live forever returned to me. I was so absorbed by the ageless perpetual rhythms I was witnessing, I had to take a deep breath to let go. Then, without warning, I recognized I was standing in the presence of God and eternity.

While standing on the beach, I recalled an experience I had in college. Students were invited to contribute writings to be published in a campus literary book called "Grain of Sand." There, in America's heartland, far from the ocean's roar, I was subtly introduced to what I would later learn was William Blake's poem:

"To see the world in a grain of sand and heaven in a wild flower
Is to hold infinity in the palm of your hand and eternity in an hour."

The words of Augustine and Blake cause me to wonder at the potential each of us possesses, and how well we are discovering ways to nurture it.

Take care of each moment and you will take care of all time.

— Buddha

Thread

The fabric was soft
Delicate, Separate, Scrap

The thread went through
Held, Strong, Protected, Woven

Ready for the next
Taken care, Held together

The thread began anew
A fresh piece, Again, Connected
Strong, Smoothed, Strengthened

The quilt is the sum
Taken care, Interwoven by thread
Intention, Awareness
To behold

August 29

Echoes of . . . Wonder

Children can teach us how to live in wide-eyed wonder.

Thinking back on this week,
> How were you lead into wonder?
> What filled you with wonder and delight?
> What did you learn from living within the wonder?

August 30

Pondering . . . Listen and Live

Listen, so that you may live.
> *(Isaiah 55:3, NRSV)*

How has your summer of listening brought you new life?
What wisdom or blessings has the summer of listening offered you?
How has a summer of listening nourished your spirit?

Blessings as you continue your journey!

Every day I see or hear something that more or less kills me with delight.

— Mary Oliver

Is it really that easy? Is God that accessible? We walk in the world with the ability to see...but really not seeing. We move around within life with ears to hear...but we are deaf to creation that calls to us, "Listen! Come see!"

We are gifted everyday with "God-art," with "God-symphonies:" a gentle breeze kissing our face...the potential in a toddler's babble... tear touching tear in a grief-induced embrace. An "ah-ha" moment birthed in a student...a canopy of color dancing in autumn winds...a friend-shared belly laugh. A butterfly floating in the air outside the window...conversation weaving itself into friendship...a walk in the woods...the heartbeat of city life. Everyday, this is God's promise: reliability, certainty, covenant. Listen.

And what of the risk of opening ourselves to God in the world among us...in us?

Well, there are worse things than dying by the hand of delight. If we willingly take the risk to acknowledge the movement of God in our everyday lives, we may find ourselves on the other side of this kind of dying, in fields of delight—dancing, laughing, singing...dying from Holy delight.

Do we want to be "killed with delight?" Once we start noticing God in the everydayness of life, life as we know it will never be the same.

In Gratitude

A large, dedicated group of people, listed below, came together to bring this book to life. The reflections were written by 44 writers, from various walks of life, from all over the United States and as far away as Australia. Five editors, five proofreaders, and one graphic designer also offered their time, talent, and enthusiasm to make this dream a reality. It has been a great pleasure and a real honor to work with everyone associated with the production of this book.

-Kathy Baker

Franklin Adkinson
Anonymous
Barbara Bachur
Virginia Barnhart
Mimi Bourgeois
Karen Brown
Mitchell Brown
Tina Brown
JoAnn Burke
Annette Chappell
Judith Cloughen
Greg Cochran
Sutton Dischinger
Cheryl Duvall
Patricia Edlund
Patricia Fosarelli
John Frisch
Robert Glushakow
Caroline Gonya
Sherry Goodill
Kerry Graham
Rebekah Hatch
Ellen Hoitsma
Mabeth Hudson
Elaine Ireland

Patricia Jackson
Patricia Kirk
Lori Lucas
Pamela McGinnis
Cathy McNally
Kathy McNany
Debbie McQuillen
Courtney Muller
Joe Muth
Carol Nemeroff
Anne Pidcock
Mari Quint
Whitney Ransome
Patty Rath
Amy Schmaljohn
Peggy Shouse
Becky Slater
Scott Slater
Ben Smith
Bob Smith
Grace Smith
Anne Sonntag
Sandy Towers
Jane Woltereck
Doris Zimmerman

Works Cited

May 31- June 6

Holy Bible. New York: HarperCollins, 1993.

Lindahl, Kay, and Amy Schnapper. *Practicing the Art of Listening: A Guide to Enrich Your Relationships and Kindle Your Spiritual Life.* Woodstock: Skylight Paths, 2003.

St. Benedict, Thomas Moore, and Timothy Frye. *The Rule of St. Benedict.* Collegeville: Order of St. Benedict, 1981.

Vaughan-Lee, Llewellyn. *Circle of Love.* Inverness: Golden Sufi Center, 1999.

Williamson, Marianne. *Illuminata: A Return to Prayer.* New York: Berkley Publishing Group, 1994.

Holy Bible. New York: HarperCollins, 1993.

June 7-13

Safransky, Sy. *Sunbeams: Sages, Saints and Lovers Celebrate the Human Heart.* Berkeley: Sun Publishing, 1990.

Hay, John. *The Immortal Wilderness.* Markham: Penguin Books, 1987.

Merton, Thomas. *Collected Poems of Thomas Merton.* New York: New Directions, 1980.

Oliver, Mary. *New and Selected Poems: Volume One.* Boston: Beacon Press, 1992.

Holy Bible. New York: HarperCollins, 1993.

June 14-20

Granat, Helen. *Wisdom Through the Ages: Book Two.* Victoria: Tafford Publishing, 2003.

Holy Bible. Grand Rapids: Zondervan, 1995.

Wiederkehr, Macrina. *The Song of the Seed: The Monastic Way of Tending the Soul.* New York: Harper Collins, 1995.

Chittister, Joan. *Illuminated Life: Monastic Wisdom for Seekers of Light.* Maryknoll: Orbis Books, 2000.

Oliver, Mary. *Red Bird: Poems.* Boston: Beacon Press, 2008.

June 21-27

Wicks, Robert. *Seeds of Sensitivity*. Notre Dame: Ave Maria Press, 1995.

Bourgeault, Cynthia. *Centering Prayer and Inner Awakening*. Cambridge: Cowley Publications, 2004.

L'Engle, Madeline. *Walking on Water: Reflections on Faith and Art*. Colorado Springs: Shaw Books, 2001.

Randolph, David James. *Candles in the Dark, Flames for the Future: Preaching and Poetry in Times of Crisis*. Berkeley: General Printing Company, 2003.

Nepo, Mark. *Exquisite Risk: Daring to Live an Authentic Life*. New York: Harmony Books, 2005.

June 28-July 4

Muller, Wayne. *Sabbath: Finding Rest, Renewal, and Delight in Our Busy Lives*. New York: Bantam Books , 1999.

Disraeli, Benjamin. *Tancred Volume I: Or the New Crusade*. Charleston: Bibliolife, 2007.

Merton, Thomas, and Christine M. Bochen. *Thomas Merton: Essential Writings (Modern Spiritual Masters Series)*. Maryknoll: Orbis Books, 2000.

Roy, Denise. *My Monastery is a Minivan: Where the Daily is Divine and the Routine Becomes Prayer*. Chicago: Loyola Press, 2001.

Kitagawa, John E. "Here I Am, Servant of the Lord." St. Philips in the Hills Parish, Tucson. 1 June 2008.

July 5-11

Gandhi, Mahatma, Louis Fischer, and M.K. Gandhi. *The Essential Gandhi: An Anthology of His Writings on His Life, Work and Ideas*. New York: Vintage Books, 2002.

Rumi, Mawlana Jalal al-Din. *Masnavi I Ma'navi*. New York: Adamant Media Corporation, 2006.

Remen, Rachel Naomi. *Kitchen Table Wisdom: Stories that Heal*. New York: Riverhead Books, 2006.

Marks, Dara Ph. D. *Inside Story: The Power of the Transformational Arc*. Studio City: Three Mountain Press, 2007.

Palmer, Parker. *Let Your Life Speak: Listening for the Voice of Vocation.* San Francisco: Jossey-Bass, 2000.

July 12-18

Genn, Robert. "Trust Art Quotes." The Painter's Keys. 30 Mar. 2009. <http://www.quote.robertgenn.com>.

Osborn, Diane K. *Reflections of the Art of Living: A Joseph Campbell Companion.* New York: Harper Collins, 1991.

Welty, Eudora, Richard Ford, and Michael Kreyling. *Eudora Welty: Stories, Essays, and Memoir.* New York: Literary Classics of the United States, 1998.

Thurman, Howard. *Footprints of a Dream.* New York: Harper, 1959.

Salzberg, Sharon. *The Kindness Handbook: A Practical Companion.* Boulder: Sounds True, Inc., 2008.

July 19-25

Smith, Robert Lawrence. *A Quaker Book of Wisdom: Life Lessons in Simplicity, Service, and Common Sense.* New York: William Morrow, 1998.

Brussat, Frederick, Mary Ann Brussat, and Thomas Moore. *Spiritual Literacy: Reading the Sacred in Everyday Life.* New York: Touchstone, 1998.

De Vinck, Catherine. *Poems of the Hidden Way.* Allendale: Alleluia Press, 1991.

O'Donohue, John. *Anam Cara: A Book of Celtic Wisdom.* New York: Harper Collins, 1998.

Silverstein, Shel. *Falling Up.* New York: Harper Collins Childrens Books, 1996.

July 26-August 1

Chittister, Joan. *Listen with the Heart, Sacred Moments in Everyday Life.* Lanham: Sheed and Ward, 2003.

Myss, Caroline M. *Invisible Acts of Power: Channeling Grace in Your Everyday Life.* New York: Simon and Schuster, 2004.

Lewis, C.S., and Clyde S. Kilby. *A Mind Awake: An Anthology of C.S. Lewis.* New York: Harcourt, Brace and World, 1969.

Calaprice, Alice, Freeman Dyson, and Albert Einstein. *New Quotable Einstein.* Princeton: Princeton University Press, 2005.

O'Donohue, John. *Anam Cara: A Book of Celtic Wisdom.* New York: Harper Collins, 1998.

August 2-8

Wheatley, Margaret J. *Turning to One Another: Simple Conversations to Restore Hope to the Future.* San Francisco: Berrett-Koshler Publishers, 2002.

Menninger, Karl. *Love Against Hate.* Orlando: Harcourt Brace Jovanovich, 1970.

Wheatley, Margaret J. *Turning to One Another: Simple Conversations to Restore Hope to the Future.* San Francisco: Berrett-Koshler Publishers, 2002.

Spangler, David. *Parent as Mystic, Mystic as Parent.* New York: Riverhead Books, 1998.

Nepo, Mark. *Facing the Lion, Being the Lion: Finding Inner Courage Where it Lives.* San Francisco: Conari Press, 2007.

August 9-15

Oliver, Mary. *Red Bird: Poems.* Boston: Beacon Press, 2008.

Bruteau, Beatrice. *Radical Optimism: Practical Spirituality in an Uncertain World.* New York: Cross Roads Publishing, 1996.

Smith, Robert Lawrence. *A Quaker Book of Wisdom: Life Lessons in Simplicity, Service, and Common Sense.* New York: William Morrow, 1998.

Holy Bible. Grand Rapids: Zondervan, 1995.

Rupp, Joyce. *The Cup of Our Life: A Guide for Spiritual Growth.* Notre Dame: Ave Maria Press, 1997.

August 16-22

Siegel, Bernie S. *Prescriptions for the Soul: Daily Messages of Inspiration, Hope and Love.* Novato: New World Library, 2004.

Genn, Robert. "Trust Art Quotes." *The Painter's Keys*. 30 Mar. 2009.
    <http://www.quote.robertgenn.com>.
Jeffers, Susan. *Feel the Fear...Do It Anyway*. New York: Ballentine
    Books, 2007.
Nouwen, Henri J.M., and Michael Ford. *The Dance of Life: Weaving
    Sorrows and Blessings into One Joyful Step*. Notre Dame: Ave
    Maria Press, 2005.
Siegel, Bernie S. *Prescriptions for the Soul: Daily Messages of Inspiration,
    Hope and Love*. Novato: New World Library, 2004.

August 23-29

Milne, A.A. *Pooh's Little Instruction Book*. New York: Dutton, 1995.
Oliver, Mary. *Why I Wake Early*. Boston: Beacon Press, 2004.
Mayer, Jerry, and John P. Holms. *Bite-Size Einstein: Quotations On Just
    About Everything from the Greatest Mind of the Twentieth
    Century*. New York: Gramercy Books, 2003.
Riffey, Cleo S. *Transforming Stress to Wonder: The Wondershift Technique*.
    Bloomington: 1st Books, 2003.
Orend, Jane. *Success Takes Practice: Inspirational Stories and Simple
    Strategies to Achieve Your Dreams*. Waterloo: Working
    Lifestyles Research and Training, 2008.

August 30-31

Holy Bible. Grand Rapids: Zondervan. 1989.
Cook, John, Steve Deger and Leslie Ann Gibson. *The Book of Positive
    Quotations, 2nd ed.*. Minneapolis: Fairview Press, 2007.

INDEX OF THEMES

Notes

Daily Listening: *A Summer of Reflection*

Notes

Notes

Daily Listening: *A Summer of Reflection*

Notes

Notes